Nora Begona

Alice in Wonderland

Enchanted Time
Coloring Book

Printed in the United States of America
First Printing, 2015

The 3Hares Castle Publishing
Houston- Buenos Aires

This Book belongs to

Hidden inside this book

These are some of the hidden objects you may find,
to make it more challenging, these are generic objects,
images would be different in the illustrations, and you may find some
more.

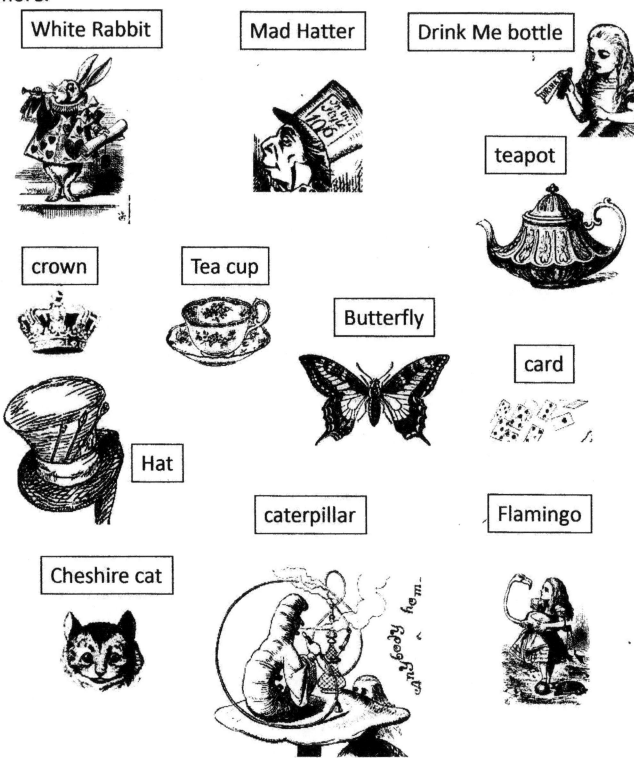

White Rabbit

Mad Hatter

Drink Me bottle

teapot

crown

Tea cup

Butterfly

card

Hat

caterpillar

Flamingo

Cheshire cat

Introduction

Alice in Wonderland Enchanted Time is : A Coloring Book of the first in a series of The Three Hares publications. In this volume, I've combined the surging popularity of grown-up coloring books with my natural instinct to draw and one of my favorite books: Alice in Wonderland. Each spread has hand-drawn images to color combined with magical illustrations from John Tenniel. You have 14 hand drawn illustrations plus 8 vintage ones. This 45page book is the perfect place to color, relaxing and celebrate your creative journey!

WOULD YOU LIKE AN
ADVENTURE NOW,
OR SHALL WE HAVE
OUR TEA FIRST?

- ALICE IN WONDERLAND

Who in the world am I?
Ah, that's the Great Puzzle.

Someone has
stolen three of
my tarts!

FOLLOW THE WHITE RABBIT

Begin
at the beginning and

go on till you

come to the end: then

Stop

Curiouser and Curiouser

IT'S
TEA TIME

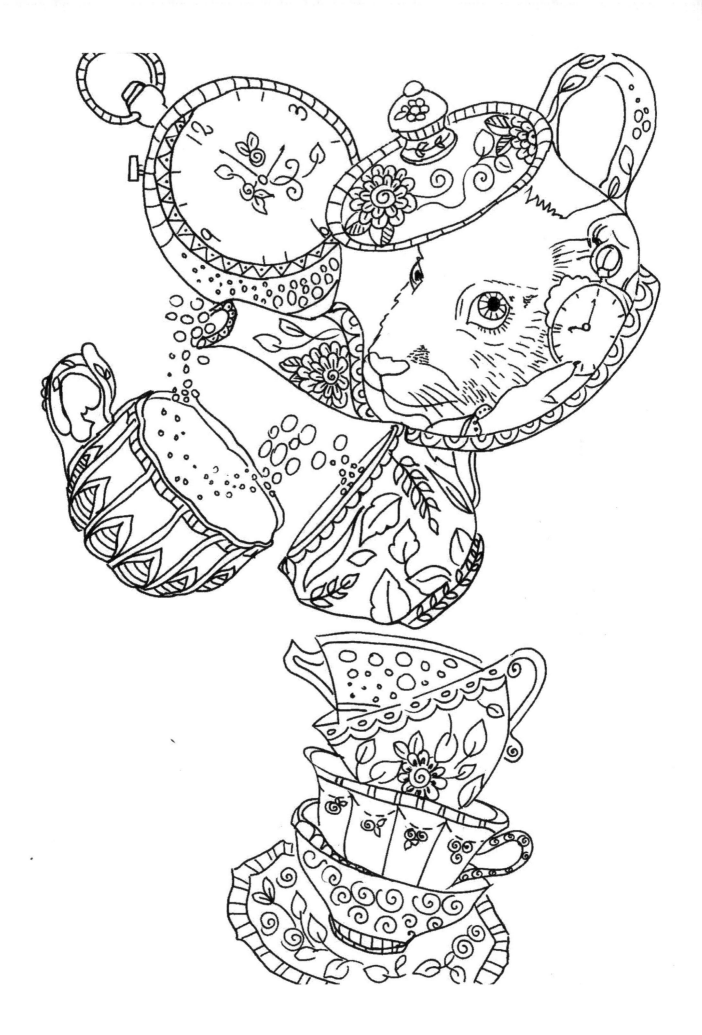

"curiouser
and
curiouser..."

lewis-carroll.tumblr.com

Who in the world am I?
Ah, that's the Great Puzzle.

Made in United States
Orlando, FL
07 October 2024

52432136R00026